A sister is friendship, fun, and family all rolled into one beautiful person. She's everything special to your heart and the dearest friend you'll ever have.

— Barbara J. Hall

Other Titles in This Series:

223 Great Things About Mothers

223 Great Things Teens Should Do

223 Great Things to Always Remember

We wish to thank Rachel Snyder, Lisa Truesdale, and the Blue Mountain Arts creative staff for contributing writings to this collection.

We gratefully acknowledge permission granted by Donna Fargo to reprint "Sisters are connected at the heart...." Copyright © 2002 by PrimaDonna Entertainment Corp. And Jacqueline Schiff for "The bond of love you share...." Copyright © 2009 by Jacqueline Schiff. All rights reserved.

Library of Congress Control Number: 2008939181
ISBN: 978-1-59842-365-5

Printed in China.
First Printing: 2009

♲ This book is printed on recycled paper.

This book is printed on fine quality, laid embossed, 80 lb. paper. This paper has been specially produced to be acid free (neutral pH) and contains no groundwood or unbleached pulp. It conforms with the requirements of the American National Standards Institute, Inc., so as to ensure that this book will last and be enjoyed by future generations.

Blue Mountain Arts, Inc.
P.O. Box 4549, Boulder, Colorado 80306

223

Great Things About

SISTERS

Blue Mountain Press ™

Boulder, Colorado

SISTERS
Are Great
Because...

🌸 They are a source of joy and happiness.

🌸 They're listeners and confidantes.

🌸 They know you and love you no matter what.

🌸 They're your favorite people in the world.

Sisters are...

❋ Commiserators.

❋ Best friends.

❋ Unique individuals.

❋ Allies.

❋ Clowns.

❋ Instigators.

❋ Shopping buddies.

❋ Intellectuals.

❋ Athletes.

❋ Angels.

❀ Sisters save the day... they are heroes.

❀ Sisters act like you sometimes...
they are mirrors.

❀ Sisters show you another side
of yourself... they are alter egos.

❀ Sisters stand up for you... they
are advocates.

❀ Sisters anticipate your next thought...
they are soul mates.

A sister is love mixed with friendship and a million favorite memories that will always last. She is a hand within yours, enfolded with hope and understanding. She gives you a feeling that makes you wonder what you would ever do without her.

— Carey Martin

❋ Your sister will be there for you no matter what — in the boring times, the exciting times, and all the moments in between.

❋ She's as dependable as the sun rising, the grass growing, and the seasons changing.

❋ You can call her anytime and know... help is on the way.

Your sister will surprise you with...

❉ A card or fresh flowers to lift your spirits when no one else knows you need it.

❉ Photographs of a recent family gathering that you wanted copies of.

❉ A CD of songs she thinks you'll like.

❉ A T-shirt from the concert you weren't able to attend.

❉ A loaf of homemade banana bread fresh from the oven.

❋ You can always be yourself around your sister.

❋ You can ask her anything or say anything to her.

❋ You can act like a kid around your sister.

❋ Sisters share a special connection, a kind of ESP (Extra Sisterly Perception).

❋ A sister is better than the world's best security blanket.

❋ She's wiser than a therapist.

❋ She's more entertaining than a good book.

❋ She's sweeter than the tastiest chocolate.

❋ She's worth more than all the money in the world.

She's got more *style*
than a personal shopper.

❉ Your sister probably knows more about you than you do.

❉ She senses when it's time to bring out the old movies and the big box of tissues.

❉ She knows when to give advice and when to just listen.

❋ Only a sister will burst out laughing with you while everyone else in the room just stares.

❋ Only a sister is able to finish your sentence after you've only uttered the first few words.

❋ Only a sister can predict you're going to call before you even pick up the phone and dial!

You and your sister go together
like peanut butter and jelly...

You're great on your own,
but together you're amazing.

❊ People can't tell your voice apart from your sister's, and it makes you both smile.

❊ A sister knows the words to your favorite song and will sing it with you.

❊ She won't bug you with stuff you're tired of hearing about.

❊ Together, sisters can face anything that life throws their way.

❋ Sisters make time to be with
you when you need them,
no matter how busy or hectic
their lives are.

❋ They give you a ride when
your car breaks down.

❋ Sisters will tell you when they
think you're heading down the
wrong road.

❋ They'll come over in the middle
of the night if you call because
you heard a strange noise and
you're scared.

❉ Your sister will head up to the mountains with you, even though she'd really rather go to the city.

❉ She'll join you for Chinese, even though she has a hankering for Italian.

❉ She'll go to the ballet with you, even though she prefers the theater.

❉ She'll go out dancing with you, even though she feels like staying in.

*S*isters are connected at the heart, and their loyalty to one another is permanent. No one can ever break that bond. They don't give up on each other easily. They have the utmost sensitivity and compassion for one another because they were born into the same family. They teach each other lessons as they stand by each other in life, and they are there for each other through everything that matters.

— Donna Fargo

✳ Sisters want you to do well in life.

✳ A sister will give you a hard
time if you're not reaching your
potential... and push you to
realize your dreams.

✳ Sisters willingly share their knowledge
about cooking, fashion, men, and life.

✳ They celebrate your
accomplishments with you.

❊ Your sister might say no when you first ask to borrow something, but then she'll lend it to you anyway.

❊ She'll fill in as your date if you don't have one.

❊ She'll clip a coupon for you for your favorite store.

❊ She'll volunteer to babysit so you can go out to dinner and a movie with your husband.

❈ Your sister will help you clean your house when unexpected guests are on their way.

❈ She'll pick you up at the airport at midnight.

❈ She'll water your plants and care for your pets while you're away.

❈ She's done so many great things for you that you've lost count.

✳ A sister is one of the only people you can trust to answer honestly when you ask, "Does this make me look fat?"

✳ She is the only person on earth you'd let in the dressing room while you try on bathing suits.

✳ She'll tell you if you have food stuck between your teeth, if your hair is sticking up, or if the tag on your shirt is showing.

Sisters will eat salad with you
if you're on a diet...

or indulge in ice cream
with you if you need a treat.

- Sisters are reliable buddies.
- They will run errands with you.
- When you feel like changing your hairstyle, they'll look through magazines with you for ideas.
- They will help you pick out a gift for your mother.

✳ Sisters offer companionship.

✳ They can gab for hours.

✳ They go to the movies with you.

✳ They understand when you're running late.

✳ They always save you a seat.

�֍ A sister reminds you of all the times you got away with doing something you shouldn't have.

✤ She was a part of the fun you had as a child... the games you played in the back of the car, time spent watching your favorite TV shows on the couch, and all your cherished summertime adventures.

✤ On family vacations, you could always count on your sister to hang out with you.

When you've got a sister...

there's a piece of you
that never grows up.

Sisters are great...

❊ Secret-handshake inventors.

❊ Gooey-brownie bakers.

❊ Board-game players.

❊ Laughing-fit starters.

❊ Funny-face makers.

❊ Birthday-party planners.

❊ Cute-outfit designers.

❋ When you're bored, you can count on your sister to come up with fun things to do.

❋ Anytime, anyplace, your sister is always up for a game of rock/paper/scissors.

❋ The two of you make terrific dance partners.

❋ Sisters are excellent companions on road trips.

Sisters can be sweet sometimes and not so sweet other times. They can be silly and fun or serious and demanding. They can be happy and easygoing or a bit grumpy and hardheaded. But whatever words you use to describe sisters, you can never really capture their true spirit, because... a sister's true spirit is found in her sensitive and caring feelings that are there when you need them. That's just the way sisters are.

— Dena DiIaconi

❋ Somehow your sister knows when it's okay to make fun of you and when she ought to take you seriously.

❋ Sisters give all they have and then some.

❋ Your sister will catch you if you fall. (And if she can't, she'll at least help you get back up.)

❋ A sister is the first person you call when you're in need of retail therapy, because she'll not only understand, but want to come along.

Sisters have been known to...

❄ Let their sisters cheat when playing cards.

❄ Tell little white lies to keep their sisters out of trouble.

❄ Set aside their own happiness to see their sisters happy.

❄ Bear a bit of discomfort so their sisters don't have to.

❄ Do a "happy dance" when their sisters need a laugh.

❊ Your sister takes your side when no one else will.

❊ She wouldn't dream of telling Mom what you really did on prom night.

❊ With all the dirt you have on your sister, you could blackmail her if you wanted... but it's much more fun to kid her about it instead.

❈ Sisters speak their own language.

❈ If you're not being entirely honest, your sister can see right through you.

❈ She'd never intentionally do anything to hurt you.

❈ A sister is someone you can trust.

With a sister, you can share
your deepest secrets.

Sisters share...

- ❉ Friends.

- ❉ Toys.

- ❉ Good times.

- ❉ Advice.

- ❉ Chores.

- ❉ Stories.

- ❉ Insights.

- ❉ Smiles.

✣ Sisters are always up on the latest gossip.

✣ They're artistic and down to earth.

✣ Sisters are tough and sweet.

✣ They're smart.

✣ And they're pretty, too.

*Sisters are the treasures of life —
they share their sunlight and part
each other's clouds. Sisters love us
always just as we are. They bring out
life's joys one star at a time.*

— *Linda E. Knight*

❋ A sister has a sparkle in her eye.

❋ A sister has plans and ideas.

❋ A sister inspires and motivates.

❋ A sister is a calming force.

❋ A sister is a voice of wisdom.

✿ Having a sister doubles your wardrobe. She'll let you borrow her jewelry, her shoes, and even her favorite LBD (Little Black Dress).

✿ Sisters will go in with you on the super-large-sized bottle of your favorite shampoo.

✿ Sisters will split an entrée with you when you're not hungry enough to eat the whole thing.

❋ Sisters always answer the phone when you call, even if they're watching their favorite TV show.

❋ They drop in for impromptu visits.

❋ They'll share the extra tomatoes, zucchinis, and lettuce growing in their gardens.

❋ When you return from vacation, they're the first ones to call and ask if you had a good time.

❋ Sisters care about your well-being.

❋ They'll bring you soup when you're sick and then stay and watch *Friends* reruns with you.

❋ They'll help you out in a pinch.

❋ They'll do favors for you — no questions asked.

A sister will call on your birthday...

to sing "Happy Birthday"
over the phone.

❄ A sister knows what your favorite color is.

❄ She's aware of your pet peeves.

❄ She remembers the story of your first kiss.

❄ She would never tell anyone else about your most embarrassing moment.

❄ She knows how to make a cup of coffee exactly the way you like it.

❋ Your sister has been a part
of some of the most important
moments in your life.

❋ When it comes to family lore
and legend, your sister is a walking
encyclopedia.

❋ She'll go to garage sales with you.

❋ She'll wallpaper your kitchen
with you.

The weather changes. The world changes. People and times change, as well. But the one thing that remains forever constant in life is a sister.

— *Elle Mastro*

❈ Sisters are steadfast, loyal,
and true.

❈ They'd travel around the
world for you.

❈ They say "I love you" even when
they're mad at you.

❈ A sister never ages —
at least not in your eyes.

- Magically, your sister can tell when you've been crying.

- Amazingly, your sister senses when you've met someone *really* special.

- Miraculously, your sister knows when you've splurged and you're feeling guilty.

- Intuitively, your sister detects when you've got exciting news to share.

✷ A sister teaches you things
you might not have learned
on your own.

✷ She's a sounding board for
bouncing off new ideas.

✷ When it comes to the most
important facets of your life,
you trust your sister's judgment
as you trust your own.

❋ Sisters are reflections of your own beauty.

❋ Sisters brush the hair out of each other's eyes.

❋ Sisters are there to accentuate the highs and elevate the lows.

❋ A sister's smile assures you that everything will be all right.

Sisters spread sunshine wherever they go.

❉ Sisters don't judge each other.

❉ A sister doesn't care what your job is, how much you make, or what kind of car you drive.

❉ A sister doesn't mind if your kitchen is dirty or the floors need sweeping.

❉ You never have to worry about what you look like when your sister is around.

❋ Sisters understand where you're coming from... or at least try to.

❋ They forgive each other faster than they'd forgive anyone else.

❋ Sisters can disagree... they can argue... they can even say mean things... but in the end, they'll be right back where they started: as friends.

The bond of love you share with a sister is strengthened by all the fond recollections of milestones in your lives. It is as unbreakable as the courage she has given you when you faced challenges together. It shines with pride in you. It holds you tight day and night and never outgrows its closeness to you. It is a priceless gift because it comes from her heart.

— Jacqueline Schiff

✳ Your sister knows about the experiences (good and bad) that have shaped your life and made you the person you are.

✳ A sister is a source of strength.

✳ Your sister feels your pain, your sorrow, your hopes, and your fears as if they were her own.

✳ You look up to your sister... and she looks up to you.

- Ask your sister if she remembers the time when…, and she'll answer, "Of course."

- Tell your sister you're sorry for that messy situation way back when, and she'll say, "You can let it go now."

- Remind your sister that you love her like no other, and she'll respond softly, "I love you, too."

❁ When your sister raises her eyebrow in a particular way, you know exactly what she's thinking.

❁ When your sister says, "Oh, you know what I mean" — you do.

❁ When your sister gives you driving directions, you understand them.

✳ A sister is your coach, mentor, cheerleader, and fan-club president all rolled into one.

✳ She glows with pride when she talks about you — whether or not you're in the room.

✳ She prays for you, hopes for you, and dreams for you... always.

A sister helps you
spread your wings and soar.

❖ A sister can laugh with you just as easily as she can laugh at you.

❖ Sisters tell hilarious jokes.

❖ Together, you can be silly.

❖ Together, you can be serious.

❋ Without sisters, family reunions might never happen.

❋ Without sisters, brothers would have no one to tease.

❋ Sisters give you nieces and nephews.

❋ When you're telling stories about your childhood, you can count on your sister to fill in the blanks.

Sisters give you treasured
lifelong memories.

❋ They're the only people on the planet who *really* understand what it was like to grow up in your family.

❋ They share the same holiday traditions as you.

❋ Sisters are a link to your past.

❋ They help you realize where you have yet to travel.

✲ A sister is fluffing up the pillows
in the guest room — before you
even buy your ticket.

✲ Sisters know and love you in a way
your husband or your partner
or your best friend never will.

✲ Sisters get what you mean
even when you can't quite put
it into words.

❃ Sisters will lend you their favorite books.

❃ They'll share recommendations with you for doctors, dentists, and hairdressers.

❃ They'll tell you if you're wearing too much makeup.

❃ They'll be maid of honor in your wedding.

❃ They'll take a yoga class with you.

Each morning when the day begins,
when other friendships fade or end,
sisters are forever.
Seasons come and seasons go,
summer rains turn into snow.
But no matter where you live...
or how far you go...
sisters are forever.

— Ashley Rice

✳ When people ask if you are sisters
or just best friends, you and your
sister answer, "Yes."

✳ Your sister unabashedly honors
and celebrates your life — even
though it may be the total
opposite of her own.

✳ Your sister respects the choices
you've made (well, at least most
of them).

✳ No matter how many miles
apart they may be, sisters are
connected with an invisible
and unbreakable golden cord.

A sister's love...

❉ Is rooted in shared experiences, family, and friendship.

❉ Only grows stronger through the years.

❉ Comforts you in the worst of times.

❉ Brings out the best in you.

❉ Follows you wherever you go.

❉ Boosts your confidence.

❉ Makes an ordinary day so
much better.

❉ Holds a special place in your
heart forever.

Sisters are one of life's greatest gifts.